THE GOTHIC LADY (LOVE STORY)

THE GOTHIC LADY (LOVE STORY)

JO JO GRAY

Contents

1

The Gothic Lady
(Love Story)

By: Jo Jo Gray

Contributed By: Jo Ann Atcheson Gray

Published by: Jo Ann Gray

The Gothic Lady

(Love Story)

I'm JoAnna Lynn. I'm petite with brown eyes and black, lengthy hair. I've always been smaller than most of the girls my age, but I manage. I'm still in high school but this should be my final year. Yes, I am a senior. I will be glad when this school year is over with. I just turned eighteen a few weeks ago, so, I'm ready to leave my parent's house and start a new life of my own.

Some would call me 'gothic', but I feel like I'm just a normal girl with 'dark' desires. Some days I feel misunderstood, especially by my parents and most of the teenagers at school. I usually stay to myself until some punk or jerk wants to try and 'pick' on me. Then I lose my temper a little and get sent home for three days. Don't mistaken me, I try to avoid any kind of conflict or arguments, but sometimes it just isn't an option.

I grew up in Central Alabama, a Southern state. I suppose I would be considered a country girl, yet I do not think I am. I've always felt I was born in the wrong town. I was not interested in the boys at my school and the girls were too 'shiny' for me. They played sports and hung out on weekends drinking beer and talking about hunting while the girls dreamed of marriage and such. I merely dreamed of leaving and seeing new places. My only hobby consisted of growing roses, mostly black and burgundy ones. I loved the roses of these colors! I planted several in my backyard and I talk to them on a daily basis. The other teenagers in town think I'm 'weird' but I don't mind. Only my roses comfort my dark soul.

I wasn't always so dark in appearance. It all began when my mother passed away last year. The pain and the sadness in my heart was unbearable, so I covered my sorrow with darkness. It was better than going into a deep depression. My father's new wife is nice, but I still cannot accept her. She wants me to be more like her with name brand clothes and stylish haircuts. I continuously refuse.

One rainy school day is when I met him, Christopher. He was adorable, different than the other guys. He was from New Orleans and just moved here with his uncle. He was tall and slender with dark brown hair that hung over his left eye, which were a bright blue. He wore blue jeans with holes in the knees and black t-shirts. He was a quiet guy with a mysterious character.

After bumping into him in the hallway and knocking my books to the floor, it all started from there. I knew I wanted him! His smile brightened my dark heart! As days went on, Christopher and I began to get closer to each other. We hung out all the time, mostly at his uncle's house, watching scary movies, listening to crazy music, and eating whatever we decided to be good at the time. I felt a slight happiness arise within me whenever he was around. He expressed to me how much he loved my attire and my way of dressing.

I often wore silly clothes such as evening gowns of dark colors with combat boots, and I usually kept mt hair piled messy on the top of my head. Normally, I would keep a black rose in my hair or whatever color I felt that day. My makeup was also darker, especially on my eyes. I felt safe, like no one could really see me behind my makeup.

Christopher would make promises of leaving this town and taking me with him. He swore to me that after graduation he would get me out of this place so we could be happy. I strangely believed him. My father did not care for him, but I didn't give a shit. Christopher was mine and we were going to be together.

My father would preach to me about Christopher and how he was just going to hurt me, but I knew he was only worried since he may lose his daughter to someone else. My father often drilled me about 'drugs' and 'sex' but I already knew of such things! I assure you I did not do drugs, but the sex I did do with Christopher. It was safe and of course I knew how to keep from getting pregnant. I wasn't stupid! I was a girl who hated alcohol, so parties were not on my agenda.

Several months blew by and Christopher bought a car. It was an old mustang that his uncle helped him purchase for his nineteenth birthday. It was bright red which made me gag but at least it rode good. On the weekends, we would venture to various places and explore different parks and movie theaters. It was such a nice time in my life!

When school finally ended and it was time for me to graduate, I did not go. I waited for my diploma to come in the mail. I was too busy with Christopher and making our preparations to leave. We agreed on going to his hometown in New Orleans. He explained to me that his grandmother, called Susie, lived in the French Quarter on the end of Royal Street. I was so excited to see a new place!

After intense arguments with my father, I finally won. So, me and Christopher loaded our baggage and set out for the French Quarter. I couldn't wait to see this place and meet Susie! Christopher assured me that his grandmother was going to love me! He told me all about her on the ride.

When we arrived that late evening at his grandmother's place in the French Quarter, it was amazing! It was an old dwelling yet beautiful. Susie owned a novelty shop with various trinkets of all sorts. There was incense sticks to tie dyed shirts for tourists. After meeting Susie, I knew I was where I wanted to be. She was a small, framed lady of seventy years old with thick blonde hair piled on her head. She wore old dresses of antique design and many bangle bracelets. Her fingers were covered in faded stone rings of different colors.

After being in the French Quarter for several weeks, I grew accustomed to the ways of this place. I started a job in Christopher's grandmother's shop while he went offshore on an oil rig to work. He would return home after a few months at a time then leave again. It took some getting used to.

I was strangely happy! Susie taught me many different cultures and the history of the French Quarter. I was intrigued at the start! My favorite practices were the 'spells' and different herbal remedies. I wasn't any good with them, but it was still awesome to be a part of something.

I never liked playing with the dark magic though, it frightened me. Susie would assure me that it was fine to be cautious of such things and she never forced me to partake in those rituals.

I would meet many strangers and several locals while running the shop on a daily routine. I enjoyed talking with the people who lived here and hearing their experiences. Often my father would call and see how I was doing, and I would tell him I'm good. I never talked too long to him but at times I did miss him.

The last time I saw Christopher was the stormy night after he returned from work. We were alone in the shop while Susie slept. Christopher had purchased a small diamond ring with a black band, asking me to marry him. I said 'yes' immediately. As the days carried on, we planned our small ceremony. We were going to be married in front of the Saint Louis Cathedral by his grandmother, who was also ordained.

It was a dream come true! The wedding was simple yet amazing, romantic! I wore a white dress with lace for the first time! I had white feathers of silk throughout my piled-up hair and flip flops with pearls across the straps. My makeup was still heavy and dark. I felt like a princess! My dark soul was brightened during this time.

Our honeymoon consisted of a weekend in St. Francisville at the Myrtles Plantation. It was an adventure! This mansion was terrifying yet gorgeous. I enjoyed the tour of the place and all the tales that went along with it. We stayed on the top floor in one of the bedrooms. It was quite spooky, but I knew I was safe with Christopher. We made passionate love that night while unexplainable bumps and sounds rang throughout the house! I was so happy!

When we returned to the French Quarter on that Monday morning, Christopher had to leave again and return to his job. I was saddened but I knew I would see him in a few weeks. I was wrong!

Some days later, Susie received a call from the manager on Christopher's oil rig. Christopher was killed by an explosion on the rig. He was instantly deceased.

Susie screamed in pain as I hit my knees behind the counter, crying as hard as I could. My heart hurt so bad! This was so much more painful than when my mother passed away. Instantly, I withdrew myself back into my darkness.

After a while, the funeral procession was set, and everyone paraded down the cobblestone streets as we ventured to the graveyard to place Christopher at rest. It was a heartbreaking day!

Later that night, I discovered a note on my pillow from Susie...

Sweet JoAnna Lynn,

I grown to love you as my own child. Hope you will carry on and live a wonderful, fulfilled life. I feel my time has come to leave this world and enter the afterlife with my Christopher and his precious mother. The shop is now yours; I've left all the paperwork under the counter in the front parlor for you. Live well, my dear and keep your spirit fresh.

Susie

I was dumbfounded after reading this. I bolted to Susie's bedroom only to find her lifeless across her bed with a bottle of anti-depressants on the side table that was empty.

Another funeral to attend and I had Susie placed next to Christopher in the cemetery. I was in a deep depression by this point. I felt so alone! I knew I would stay in the French Quarter and continue to run Susie's shop, yet I felt abandoned, left behind!

A few weeks slipped by, and I discovered I was expecting a child. I controlled my depression by focusing on my baby being born. The day she arrived was beautiful! She had curly brown hair and bright blue eyes and favored her daddy quite a bit. I named her Susanna Christie. I would always honor Susie and Christopher by naming our child after them.

Time continued on as I raised my daughter here in the French Quarter. My father and his absurd wife came on many occasions to visit and see their grandchild. Susanna Christie loved them so much!

I continued to wear dark vintage clothes while I dressed my baby girl in pastel colors with lace. She was an amazing toddler and very smart! I taught all the herbal remedies that Susie had taught me, and she was quite good at performing her 'magic'. She adopted a few cats of different colors as her pets and enjoyed playing with them. They would even sleep next to her at bedtime.

So, you have my little story of my simple life. I dwell in the French Quarter still with my daughter who has grown into an amazing woman. Susanna Christie now has children of her own, four sons and one daughter, and a husband who is in the medical field. They live only miles from me outside of the French Quarter. My father passed away some months back with cancer while his awful wife moved on.

I spend my days at my shop while playing and enjoying my grandchildren on a regular routine. Life hasn't been perfect, but it has its special moments. I will carry on exactly the way Susie said in her final note to me.

The Gothic Lady
(Love Story)

The Gothic Lady (Love

More titles available online by:
Jo Ann Atcheson Gray
Jo Jo Gray
Anna Elizabeth
Sasha Joy
Published by Jo Ann Gray

The Gothic Lady
(Love Story)